Blood Pressure Guide-book

Peter Maxwell

Contents

Chapter 1

INTRODUCTION

Foods connect people from all over the world, but a poor diet can cause an individual to become overweight and obese.

This poor health condition for African-Americans is compounded by the issues of food production, and the unavailability of proper health care. Approximately 47.8% of African-Americans are obese. Obesity in this group of people is increased by the unavailability of proper nutrition. Also, 35.1% of overweight African-Americans are between the ages of 20-40.

The focus of cancer care is on prevention, with the maintenance of clean and healthy living habits also playing a key role in the reduction of cancer.

African Americans are likely to die from various types of health issues, including heart disease, stroke, diabetes, and cancer. Due to the types of foods people eat, the main health issues in this population are obesity, heart disease, stroke, and diabetes. They are often not meeting the Recommended Dietary Allowances for various nutrients. These individuals should begin eating more fruits and vegetables. Furthermore, if possible, an African American diet should

It is not easy to diagnose a chronic disease in a black adult. There are several reasons for this. In order to get a diagnosis, you must first have the money to pay for it.

If you don't want to put yourself under a weight restriction, incorporate healthy habits, which will last you a lifetime. These habits will help you look, feel, and even live better.

The Key to Eating the Foods You Love and Still Be Healthy and Fit

A study already found that African Americans were very fond of and enjoyed food. This should be a good thing, since it means that they are eating right. However, they can do better when it comes to their diets. Recipe books are available that will pass on the basics to people who are in need of a little help. Food combinations can be altered to taste better or to serve better health purposes.

Keep these few simple tips in mind, so you can eat the foods you love while staying healthy.

A single glass of one-percent or two-percent milk may not seem like very much, but it contains plenty of calcium, a key ingredient to healthy bones. Boost your food with spices: Red peppers, garlic, curry, tumeric, lemon, basil, and

Never leave a vegetable on your plate. You can steam, fry or sauté it. You can also grill, roast or boil it. Try to fill up your plate with lots of veg. 3. Salad and vegie side dishes are great: If you're the vegetarian

It is hard to turn back from meat, but use healthy meat in smaller amounts to add flavor. In place of ham hocks, you can use smoked turkey or fish, or pile on the spices.

It is common knowledge that certain cooked grains, including rice and corn, are high in fiber. To add these whole grains to your meals is a good way to improve your health over cooking. Commiting these grains in your soups, or mixing them with your beans is a good way to add these grains to your daily diet. Let your imagination

Peas and rice intermingle to make a dish that is commonly prepared throughout the globe. Put your rice and peas in bowls together and make it your new favorite meal.

Mash your sweet potatoes (or cook

Eat only healthy foods: at a shop, buy peanuts or fruit; at a little shop, load up your plate with salad, vegetables, fruit, and beans.

Fruits like melons, peaches, berries, and mangos enhance a food by adding a sweet taste to it. They can even give you a satisfying feeling after eating your meal.

Moscow Mule: A digestive beverage that includes a mix of beer and ginger ale, vodka, and lime juice. Add about 5 slices of ginger to beef up the spice.

Chapter 2

RECIPES

Chicken With black-eyed peas and yellow rice

Ingredients

· 1 Tablespoon olive oil

A cup of chopped red onion

· 1 ½ pounds chicken tenderloins

2/3 cup low-fat dairy cream

· ½ teaspoons poultry seasoning

Half to one teaspoon of ground black pepper The main point of pepper is to add flavor to your meals. You can make your meals more delicious by adding garlic, onions,

· ¼ teaspoon crushed red pepper

A mixture of yellow rice and saffron has been used for centuries.

· Bake 15 ounces of black-eyed peas. You'll need to use canned black-eyed peas--preferably 15 ounces (don't use pre-cooked dried beans). Wash and drain cans.

· 2 teaspoons fresh thyme

· Finely chopped red onion (optional)

· Snipped fresh thyme (optional)

Preparation

Prep: 10 minutes

Readying In: 35 minutes

· Add 1 teaspoon garlic powder in a bowl. · Mix with a spoon (not machine) for 3 minutes.

·

Prepare one cup rice according to the recipe.

1: Add to the pot black-eyed peas and thyme. Cover and cook about 10 minutes or until the beans and liquid are absorbed. If desired, garnish with additional finely chopped red onion and freshly chopped thyme.

TIP:

You can go out and buy yellow rice that is saffron-flavored and combine it with all the other rice you purchase. As with the Goya brand, mix the seasonings in a separate bowl, measure out a ½ cup

Nutritional information

Ø cup

Per each serving it has 276 calories, 4 grams of fat (1 gram of which is saturated), 5 grams of fiber, 28 grams of carbs, 31 grams of protein, 9 micrograms of folic acid, 66 micrograms of vitamin A, 32 micrograms of vitamin C, 32 milligrams of

Ø Carbohydrate Servings: 2

Olivia eats lunch that includes 3 lean protein and 2 starch foods.

CHICKEN IN ORANGE AND WHITE SAUCE WITH BLACK-EYED PEAS AND RICE

LEMON DREAM PIE

Ingredients

Cream Cheese Crust

¼ teaspoon cream of tartar

.75 cup of raw sugar

· ½ teaspoon vanilla extract

To make the frosting, I sifted 2 cups of confectioners' sugar to remove some of the clumps.

Lemon Filling

½ cup granulated sugar ½ cup granulated sugar

·

· 2 large eggs

The original recipe calls for six tablespoons of lemon juice for every cup of sugar.

1 teaspoon freshly grated lemon zest

2 tablespoons butter

· 1 cup fresh raspberries

For decoration:

Preparation

Prep: 45 minutes

Ready In: 2 hours and 45 minutes

To make the meringue is as follows: Preheat the oven to 275 F and line the bottom of the 9-inch pie pan with foil. Make sure to paint the foil with oil.

Fold in the confectioners' sugar when the meringue is fizzy, not after.

Make the meringue into a pie shell by spooning it into the pie dish and then, by using the back of a spoon, by hollowing out the center and spreading it upwards to form the shell.

· Bake for one hour at 250°F. Turn down the oven to 250°F and bake until the meringue is firm, dry, and just beginning to brown, 30 to 40 minutes longer. The pie will cool in the oven. To remove the meringue and foil, first place the foil-side on the counter and gently peel it

Be prepared to make a filling for pie. Mix the sugar, egg whites, lemon juice, and lemon zest in a bowl. Add the butter and fold the mixture until the butter mixture is combined with the other ingredients. Cook the filling over low heat until it thickens and bubbles several times, about 5 minutes. (The filling thickness should be thickened but not scrambled.)

· Place the cheese filling in a bowl and immediately cover it with plastic wrap to prevent it from forming a skin and refrigerate until completely chilled, about 1 hour.

In the good old days, assembling a pie used to be simple. You simply spooned the chilled lemon filling into a meringue shell, and filled the center with fresh raspberries that have been lightly (and mysteriously) "dust[ed] with confectioners

Make Ahead Tip: The pie shell may be prepared ahead and baked through Step 4. It can then be cool to refrigerate and place in an airtight container. The filling can be prepared ahead and refrigerated until just before serving.

To bring an egg to room temperature, break it in half and place one half on a plate on the counter for 15 minutes or submerge the other half in a bowl of tepid water for five minutes.

Nutrition information

0 (translating to 100)

Vitamin C (35% daily value)

Ø Carbohydrate Servings: 2½

½ cup fruit, 2 other carbohydrate

LEMON DREAM PIE!

BUTTERMILK CUSTARD PIE

Ingredients

Crust

the batter for the cupcakes contained 1 cup of all-purpose flour. 1 cup of plain yogurt Paraphrase: the frosting for the cupcakes contained 1 cup of

1 tablespoon of sugar . . . .

· ½ teaspoon salt

·

· 3 tablespoons oil

1-2 tablespoons ice water

Filling

¾ cup of sugar

¼ cup of all-purpose flour

·

·salt in a pinch

· 2 large eggs

One egg white.

· 2 cups (lightly whisked) buttermilk

· 1 tablespoon lemon zest

·

· Feeling the need for fresh fruit, making a smoothie is a good alternative.

Preparation

Prep: 45 m

30 minutes until you're ready

With flours, you can make almost any bread in your kitchen. This bread recipe doesn't need much. You can use any kind of flour. Some people go to the store and buy only white flour. There, you get a lumps. When you use whole grain, you end up with a crumblier bread.

To prepare the dough, place plastic wrap on the work surface and flatten the dough into a circle. Place inside a 9-inch pie pan. Cover with two more plastic sheets and roll the dough to a thickness of about 1/2 inch. Remove the top plastic sheets and fold the edges under at the rim of the pan. Crimp the edge. Cover with plastic and refrigerate 15 minutes.

· Butter a 9 in. pie dish or metal pie pan and line it with a crust. Wrap extra crust dough around the bottom and sides of the pan and gently press together so that it adheres to the sides and bottom. Fill the crust with the mincemeat and roll it out thinly. Bake blind until the crust is golden and the mincemeat is just set in the middle

To make a pie dough: Put the skimming of butter in a mixing bowl. Add sugar, flour, and salt. Mix together with a beater or wire whip until it forms a ball. Whisk the eggs until frothy. Add the buttermilk, lemon juice and vanilla. Mix the liquid into the flour mixture by hand. Pour into the pie shell and sprinkle the top with grated nutmeg. Bake at

Cover the edges of the crust to prevent moisture from spilling out. Bake the pie until the cheese is no longer wobbly. Cool the pie on a wire rack for 15 minutes, then refrigerate for 2 hours and serve garnished with fresh berries.

Nutrition information

Ø Carbohydrate Servings: 2½

Ø Exchanges: 2½ other carbohydrate

BUTTERMILK CUSTARD PIE

PRETZEL, COTTAGE CHEESE & CHEESE

Ingredients

· 1 pound of spicy Italian sausage With removed casings

· you can get lots of benefits from onions, such as health, money savings, and time savings.

· When carrots are soaked in water for overnight, they can be shredded in a food processor while you are in the mood for a raw carrot dish.

Eat the proper amount of salt

"Taste" suggest the "on" and "off" value of pepper,

· 3 2 pounds prepared cornbread, cut into ¾-inch cubes (about 12 cups)

·¼ cup chopped fresh parsley ¼ cup chopped fresh parsley Paraphrase: ·¼ cup chopped fresh parsley Paraphrase: ·¼ cup

· 1 tablespoon chopped fresh sage

· Semolina dough · Roasted chicken breasts Paraphrase: · Semolina dough ·

Preparation

Active: 25 m

Get in your 50 m

· Preheat oven to 325°F and coat a 9 by 13 inch pan with cooking spray.

· Add sausage, onion, celery, cornbread, parsley, sage, and salt and pepper. Let sausage and vegetables rest for ½ hour and serve.

Gingerly stir the stuffing with hot broth until it tastes right to you. Add broth as needed, so it feels moist but not wet. Hold stuffing over a cooking vessel until you think it's right, so you don't end up with wet stuffing.

Cook the stuffing until it's warmed through, about 25 minutes. Then, serve it.

Make ahead tip: If you wish to freeze and reheat the casserole, you can prepare through Step 3. Cover and refrigerate for up to 1 day. Reheat immediately in a 350° oven until hot.

Nutrition information

1 cup

Ø Per serving: 241 calories; 8 grams of fat; 2 grams fiber; 33 grams of carbohydrates; 9 grams of protein; 12 micrograms of folic acid; 28 milligrams of cholesterol; 12 grams of sugars; 7 grams of added sugars; 166 international units of vitamin A; 4 milligrams of vitamin C

Ø Carbohydrate Servings: 2

Paraphrase: Ø medium fat meat (2 starch, 1)

CORNBREAD & SAUSAGE STUFFING

PEACH-BOURBON UPSIDE-DOWN CAKE

Ingredients

· 4 cups fresh peaches (about 6 peaches) Tip: Look for some color diversity in this recipe. While peaches are delightful in their own right,

3 tablespoons of brown sugar.

· To make the aromatic herbal tea

· 1 tablespoon powdered milk

· ⅓ cup sifted cake flour

1 teaspoon baking powder can be used in your baking.

· 1 tablespoon baking powder ¼ teaspoon salt

·

⅔ cup of sugar, divided by ⅔ cup of sugar

· 2 eggs with egg whites. Check that the two sentences are 100% identical and fairly there is good English in the latter

· 1½ teaspoons vanilla extract

Preparation

Active: 30 m

Ready In: 1 hour and 30 minutes.

· Line a thin-skinned oven with foil and coat the foil with cooking spray.

Place a bowl of brown sugar, cornstarch, 1 tablespoon of bourbon, and peaches are combined in a pan.

Mix the following ingredients, in the proportions shown in a food processor: 1 cup of flour, 1/2 cup of pecans, 1/2 cup of baking powder, and 1 teaspoon of sea salt.

To create this texture, beat the egg whites and sugar in a mixing bowl with an electric mixer until soft peaks form. Gradually beat in half of the sugar, continuing to beat until the egg whites are thick and glossy, about 5 minutes. Beat the whole eggs with the remaining sugar in a second bowl until thick and pale, about 5 minutes. Beat in the remaining half of the egg whites, then the bourbon and the vanilla. In a third bowl, sprinkle the remaining flour in half and the remaining beaten eggs in the remaining half. Gently combine the flour and beaten eggs with the bourbon and vanilla in the egg-

Spread the batter in a comparable sized pie pan or bowl. Bake at 400 degrees until the top looks slightly matte and the bottem starts to flutter. The cake can be baked in a ovenproof bowl or a greased baking dish, but the high heat of the oven could lead to cracks and shrinkage in the cake. The best way to go is the standard pie pan or bowl.

Among peach-peeling tips: Boil your peaches to make them easier to peel. Immerse them in boiling water for 1 minute. Cool them in cold water, then slide off their skins with a paring knife.

To toast whole nuts: Spread nuts on a baking tray and bake at 350º F, stirring once, until fragrant, about 7-9 minutes.

Nutrition information

Per serving: 177 calories; 5 g fat (1 g sat); 2 g fiber; 31 carbohydrates; 4 g protein; vitamin A (4 mcg), vitamin C (4 mg), vitamin D (15 lU), vitamin E (21 mg), thiamin (8.1 mg), ribof

Ø Carbohydrate Servings: 2

Carbohydrate, 1 fat

Bourbon-Gooseberry Upside-Down Cake

OYSTERS ROCKEFELLER

Ingredients

Fourteen oysters and then

· spinach • 7-9 cups fresh florets picked just before cooking • 3 large kale bun

A handful of watercress leaves or more spinach.

· 1 cup handful of fresh celery (approximately 3 stalks) · 1 cup of parsley leaves

· 2 tablespoons butter

· Scallions, finely chopped.

· Pernod or other licorice-flavored liqueur (about 6 tablespoons)... Types: · Kahiki (crystal) Original: ·

· 40 drops of lemon juice

· A little bit of hot sauce.

¼ cup freshly grated Parmesan cheese

Preparation

Active: 1 h 30 m

Get going: 1 hr 45 mins

· Shuck oysters, discarding shells that have been broken. This amounts to the "liquor" left behind in the shells and the oyster meat are put into one bowl. A colander is used to strain the liquid and discard the meat. Then, oyster shells are rinsed before put away.

· . . . .

· Cook the greens with onions, until the scallions are soft and any liquid has evaporated. Add the strained oyster liquor, taste for licorice, and lemon juice; then simmer the greens until moisture has almost dissipated.

· Meanwhile, preheat oven to 450°F. Line a shallow baking pan or a baking sheet with about ½ inch of rock salt (or coarse salt) or loosely crumpled foil to make a base for the oyster shells.

. . . . For each oyster, reserve the round white part of the oyster and set aside. Empty each oyster into the prepared and cooked lobster claw, evenly divide the bake sauce among oysters and sprinkle with Parmesan. Bake until the sauce is bub

Oyster meat and liquid are only meant to be mixed together at the last minute, and these two steps allow for this. Prepare the sauce, place it in the refrigerator or freezer if it is not going to be used right away, and bring it out when needed.

Nutrition information

Approximately four Gulf oysters.

Ø Calories per serving: contains 147 calories Fat per serving: contains 7 grams of fat Carbs per serving: contains 12 grams of carbs Protein per serving: contains 6 grams of protein Folate per serving: the recommended daily intake for folate is 400 mcgs Vitamin A per serving: contains 420 IU V

Ø 70% Nutricion Service

Ø Carbohydrate Servings: ½

½ vegetable carbohydrate, 1 lean meat, 1 fat

OYSTERS ROCKEFELLER

OLD CORN

Ingredients

· 3

1 cup fresh and 1 cup frozen corn popped into a medium-sized pot.

"A teaspoon of ground pepper"

• 1 cup nonfat milk, plus more if needed

Preparation

Active: 25 m

Ready in: 25 m

· When the bacon is cooked and crisped, drain the bacon on a paper towel. Add oil to the pan again and add the corn. When the corn begins to brown, add pepper and stir the corn around.

· Add 1 cup milk to the frying pan and bring to a simmer. Stir to scrape up any browned bits. Cook at a medium simmer until all of the milk has evaporated and mixture is ketchup-like. Stir the corn to combine. Top with crumbled bacon, which will be softened. Serve.

To make ahead tip: cover and refrigerate for up to 3 days.

Nutrition information

Ø[1] Serving size: generous

One serving contains 146 calories; five grams of fat(1 gram of saturated); two grams of fiber; twenty two grams of carbs; six grams of protein; forty five milligrams of folate; four milligrams of cholic acid; fourteen hundred fifty seven hundred and eighty one international units of vitamin A; seven hundred and

Ø Carbohydrate Servings: 1½

Ø Exchanges: 1½ starches, 1 fat

OLD CORN

CHOCOLATE PUDDING

Ingredients

· 1 cup skim milk

· 116) Conclusion essay ⅓ cup packed light brown sugar 117) First paragraph ⅓ cup packed light brown sugar 118) Dedicate the first

· 1 large egg

· 3 tablespoons of unsweetened cocoa powder

· ½ cup cornstarch

· A cup of chopped chocolate chips (1 ounce).

The recipe calls for 1 teaspoon vanilla extract.

Preparation

Active: 15 m

15 Minutes ready

Heat milk, brown sugar, eggs, cocoa, and cornstarch to a boil in a medium saucepan.Cook for 3 to 5 minutes, whisking constantly.

· Mix together the pudding, cream cheese, chicken, cake, and milk in a bowl. Refrigerate until you are ready to serve it.

Nutrition information

Calcium (26% daily value)

Ø Carbohydrate Servings: 3

Ø (FIGURE : 5.58)

CHOCOLATE PUDDING

Duchess

Ingredients

· 1¾ pounds boneless, skinless chicken thighs, trimmed and cut into 1 inch pieces.

⅓cup All Purpose flour, mixed with ⅔ cup water (make sure the water adds up to the whole of the flour!)

· 2 tablespoons canola oil

· 2 large carrots, diced

·· 2 stalks celery with diced lemon juice Paraphrase: ·· 2 stalks of celery with minced lemon juice.

1 large onion 2 tomatoes, diced 1 cloves of garlic, crushed 8 cups fresh sweet corn 8 cups water 2 tsp salt 1 bay leaf 1 tsp white

You can toast skewers in a pan, and season with poultry seasoning.

· ½ teaspoon salt

"Add 2 teaspoons of freshly ground black pepper to the food."

· 2 14-ounce cans reduced-sodium chicken broth This site is a parody. If you think there's a legitimate

· 1 cup of water

· ½ cup frozen peas, thawed.

· 1 cup whole-wheat pastry flour 3 eggs 1 tablespoon butter 1/2 cup hot water

1/3 cup all-purpose flour (3 oz)

· A few pinches of ground poultry seasoning.

· ½ teaspoon baking soda.

Using

One ¼ cup nonfat buttermilk, (using ¾ cup from Tip)

Preparation

Active: 45 m

Ready to get in shape in 1 hour?

· Dredge chicken in ¾ cup flour in a medium bowl until coated. Heat 1 tablespoon oil in a Dutch oven over medium heat. Add the chicken and cook, stirring occasionally, until lightly browned, 3 to 5 minutes. Remove the chicken from the pot and transfer to a plate.

· Add 2 tablespoons flour to a 4 quart saucepan and stir. Heat over medium-low heat until boiling. Stir a heaping tablespoon of flour into the 1 tablespoon oil. Add the carrots, celery, onion, ½ teaspoon salt and pepper to the 4 quart saucepan. Stir to coat, then cover and cook until the vegetables are softened, about 5 to 7 minutes. Sprinkle the reserved

Meanwhile, mix together whole-wheat flour, all-purpose flour, poultry seasoning, baking soda, and salt in a medium bowl. Add buttermilk to the flour mixture. Mix until just combined, making a sticky dough.

The dumplings will rise while the chicken cooks, so be careful when you transfer them to the serving dish.

For those with no access to buttermilk or sour milk, there is a substitute for these common beverages: You can use powdered buttermilk, whoever prepared it according to package directions.

Nutrition information

For each serving, you get 460 calories, 14 grams of fat (3 grams of saturated fat), 6 grams of fiber, and 46 grams of carbohydrates, 34 grams of protein, 0 mcg of folate, 90 mg of cholesterol, 6 grams of sugars, 4,848 IU of vitamin A, 10 mg of vitamin C, 59 mg of

Ø Nutrition

Ø Carbohydrate Servings: 3

Extra Fat: 2½ Starch, ½ Vegetable, 3 Lean Meat, 1 Fat-Free Milk and Yogurt, 1 Fruit

Awesome Chicken and Stuffing

À la King Chicken

Ingredients

1½ pounds boneless, skinless chicken breast trimmed and cut into 1″ cubes

½ cup all-purpose flour / 1 cup rice flour

1 tablespoon canola oil, 1 tablespoon olive oil, divided.

· 10 ounces white mushrooms (roughly equivalent to six full cups of mushrooms or 10 to 12 pieces),

2 large green bell peppers, diced

Salt is a great addition to a healthy diet.

Worry about half a teaspoon of pepper, but don′t really know what it is anyway.

cup dry sherry, remove alcohol.

Your original meal is comprised of 1 cup of reduced-sodium chicken broth and 1 cup of water.

· 1 cup low fat milk

8 ounces of tomatoes with a little salt, pepper, and orange juice from one fresh orange.

· Balsamic vinegar ½ cup sliced scallions

Preparation

Active: 35 m

35 m / 1.1 km

2 tablespoon oil is added to a large skillet. 1 tablespoon of flour is added to the pan. The chicken is added to the pan, brown, and is transferred to a plate.

sauté the mushrooms and bell pepper with salt and pepper for 3 to 5 minutes. Add sherry, bring to a boil and cook, stirring to scrape up the browned bits.

Add chicken broth to flour and stir until smooth. Bring to a boil, then turn down to low, and simmer for 5 minutes. Stir in scallions.

Sherry is a type of fortified wine which is made from fermented sugarcane juice. Do not buy the "cooking" sherry sold in supermarkets because it contains too much salt. Instead, find regular dry sherry that's also found with other fortified wines in your local wine or liquor store

Nutrition information

One cup of chicken

Per: mg Protein: mcg Cholesterol: mg Carbohydrates: mg Sodium: mg Potassium: mg Vitamin A: IU Vitamin C: mg Calcium: mg Iron: mg

Ø

Ø Carbohydrate Servings: 1

Ø Exchanges: 1 starch, 3 lean meat

Slice of CASHEW CHICKEN

Chicken-Fried Steak & Gravy

Ingredients

Sift the flour.

· 2 large egg whites, lightly beaten

-½ cup corn-meal

¼ cup whole-wheat flour

1 cup plus 1 tablespoon cornstarch.

· Siracha: 1 teaspn rem

· 1 pound cube steak, cut into 4 portions

¾ teaspoon salt, ¼ teaspoon kosher salt.

A splash of hot pepperseed, paired with an even, medium-level amount of pepper, can brighten up a bowl of chili.

· 1 teaspoon canola oil · 2 tablespoons canola oil · 1 teaspoon canola oil

. A can of reduced-sodium beef broth

· 1 tablespoon water.

· ½ cup half-and-half

Preparation

Active: 35 m

Three Minute Workout

· Heat the oven to 350°F. Cook the chicken on a greased baking sheet.

Pair up the crust for the chicken breasts with the flour dusting. Pour the cornmeal into a shallow dish. Add seasonings on each side of the meat and coat. Firm up the chicken by dipping it into the remaining egg whites, then coat in the corncob mixture.

In season one of the show, his closest colleagues betray him by making moves against his family. Further betrayal touches him when his mother's friend turns informant and his kids search for information about his activities on the Internet. Season two includes an element of treachery when Tony's wife Carmela moves with her children out of the suburbs and to Tony's hometown of Meadowlands. The episodes intersperse the gang and romantic relationships to portray the deeper theme of Tony Soprano and his family in turmoil.

In other words, add the dissolved thickening agent to the hot pan and allow the mixture to thicken to a gravy consistency, about 3 to 5 minutes. Whisk the water and cornstarch until smooth. Add the cornstarch mixture to the pan; remove from the heat. Stir in half-and-half and season with salt and pepper. Serve with the thickened gravy.

To keep your baking sheets clean, spray them with cooking spray before placing the food on the foil.

Nutrition information

Ø serve

Ø Per serving: 307 calories; 12 grams of fat (3 grams saturated); 1 gram fiber; 18 grams of carbohydrates; 30 grams of protein; 19 mcg of folic acid; 83 mg of cholesterol; 1 gram of sugars; 0 grams of added sugars; 177 IU of vitamin A; 0 mg of vitamin C; 39 mg of calcium

Ø Carbohydrate Servings: 1

ø 1 starch, 3 lean meat, 1 fat

A CHICKEN-FRIED STEAK WITH GRAVY

Healthy and delicious

Ingredients

· Crust

Oil must be heated and canola oil is ideal.

Drifting along in the river of life, where was he headed?

2 teaspoons of sugar

1/2 teaspoon of baking powder

Buy salt in a fancy box, not a can.

· 4 or more cups low-fat milk

⅓ cup quick or regular rolled oats.

In 1 cup all-purpose flour, add ¼ cup

1 cup brown sugar

· ¾ - 1 tablespoons canola oil

½ tablespoon water

½ cup sugar

How to cook a bread at home

2 pounds tart apples are cut into 6 cups.

·

· You can substitute 1/2 cup of fresh or dried fruit.

Preparation

Active: 50 m

Get ready in: 2 hours and 5 minutes Note: I'd be interested to hear how this works for your audiences. A:

After preparing the crust, we stir oil and flour together and will keep them in the refrigerator until they are partially frozen.

Mix the flour, sugar, baking powder, and salt in a mixing bowl. Using a pastry blender or the back of a fork, cut the chilled butter into smaller pieces until it resembles coarse meal. Stir in the frozen butter cubes and the chilled milk, one tablespoon of the milk a time, just until a soft dough forms.

Coating the pie pan with cooking spray.

· To make topping · Combine the oats, flour and brown sugar in a small bowl with a fork or your fingers. Drizzle oil and water over the mixture and stir together to form small crumbs.

· To prepare pie: Mix the sugar and flour in a large bowl. Toss apples and cranberries with lemonspecific portion.

Roll the dough into a 12-inch circle and transfer to a prepared pie pan. Fold the edges under and pinch them to form the top crust.

"The best part is this: the top is crispy and crunchy! with no under-topping or greasy crust. It is just so moist, it's a bit chewy, it's not as sweet as apple pie, but there's no other pie like it." "My son was a fan of apple pie even before I got pregnant. He wants me

Nutrition information

This one is based on the phrase Ø Serve, which means 'not worth mentioning'. It is based on the fact that the executive chef of the restaurant serves the same menu that has been on the menu for years. This is one of the most popular dishes on the menu. It is a cheap dish, but it is a dish that you

Ø Carbohydrate Servings: 4

1 fruit, 3 other carbohydrate, 1½ fat

NO-BUTTER APPLE CRANBERRY PIE.

CURRANT SCONES

Ingredients

· 2 cups all-purpose flour

· ¼ cup light brown sugar.

1 teaspoonx of baking powder

· A tablespoon of powdered milk

Add ½ teaspoon salt

· ¾ cup buttermilk

· ⅓ cup currants

· a tablespoon of oil to cook,

· · · 1 teaspoon low fat milk to brush your teeth with.

Preparation

Active: 20 m

Start here: 35 minutes

Preheat oven to 350°F. Lightly grease a

In a large bowl, add flour, brown sugar, baking powder, cream of tartar, and salt. Stir well to combine. Add buttermilk, currants, and oil, and mix to combine. Sprinkle the buttery crumbs over the batter.

· Travel to India.

Nutrition information

A serving of the Original contains 130 calories, 2 grams of fat, 1 gram of fiber, 27 grams of carbohydrates, 3 grams of protein, and 61 milligrams of folic acid. It also contains 10 units of vitamin A, 0 units of vitamin C, 11 mg of the B12 vitamin, 51 mg of calcium, 1

Ø Carbohydrate Servings: 2

1 starch, ½ fruit

CURRANT SCONES

RUM-RAISIN BREAD PUDDING

Ingredients

½ cup raisins

· 2 tablespoons rum, or brandy.

· Four pieces of whole-grain bread, torn into small pieces.

2 large eggs

Bob made fried eggs for the kids and poured a cup of milk.

· In a large bowl, mix the brown sugar and eggs. In a separate bowl or plate, combine the flour, baking powder and salt. Pour the dry ingredients into the wet ingredients and

· 1 splatter of vanilla on top of the mixture.

· ¼ teaspoon ground nutmeg

Preparation

Active: 20 m

1 hour is the time you need to get started.

Preheat the oven to 350°

· Mix slowly 1/4 cup dark rum, (or brandy) 1/2 cup (1 full tablespoon) butter, 1 tsp vanilla extract, 1 cup brown sugar, 3 egg and 1/2 cups of pumpkin. Spread ingredients over bread in an even layer.

Whisk eggs in a medium bowl. Add evaporated milk, brown sugar, vanilla, and nutmeg; whisk until the sugar dissolves. Stir in the raisin-soaked bread pieces and let rest for 10 minutes. Pour the mixture over the bread pieces; mix with a fork. Let stand for 10 minutes.

· Bake the pudding until it is puffed and set in the center. 44

Nutrition information

'Ø'

M

Ø Carbohydrate Servings: 5

Ø Exchanges: 3½ other carbs, ½ fat

RUM-RAISIN BREAD PUDDING

BRANDIED NECTARINES

Ingredients

· ½ cup brandy, preferably Cognac

· A: I would suggest changing the order of the sentences slightly: Original: Mis/disinformation and privacy: key takeaways Paraphrase:

· A piece of vanilla bean a 1 inch long.

·....

Preparation

Active: 20 m

Ready Within 20 Minutes

Arrange brandy, sugar, and a vanilla bean in a skillet large enough to hold nectarines in one layer. Grill the nectarines over a low heat (be careful with the alcohol!). Make sure that the nectarines do not burn.

· Remove the pan from the heat. Uncover and allow the nectarines to cool a bit. Discard the skins if they are easy to remove. Transfer the nectarines cut-side up to a serving dish. Drizzle the syrup over the top. Serve warm.

Nutrition information

The food box is gender specific, with a female version containing 90 calories each and a male counterpart with 151 calories per serving.

Ø Carbohydrate Servings: 1½

Ø Exchanges: 1½ other carbohydrate

BRANDIED NECTARINES

LEMON-PEPPER CATFISH

Ingredients

(paraphrased) To start: mixing 2 tablespoons of lemon juice

· 3 ounces, extra-virgin olive oil

· 1-2 teaspoons finely crushed black peppercorns

-- ½ teaspoon salt--

4 cat fish fillets, about 1 pound total.

Cut 4, lemon wedges and squeeze one to juice. Open the juice. Barely enough for 1 teaspoon.

Preparation

Active: 45 m

48 m

Place the fish in a shallow nonreactive dish. Combine all ingredients together in a good quality blender, and then incorporate the mixture into the fish.

· Preheat the broiler or grill.

Put the fish into an oiled broiler pan, turn it once, and then leave it in there.

Fish that flakes easily requires a delicate touch to flip on the grill. To avoid overcooking, measure a piece of foil large enough to hold the fish and coat it with cooking spray. Grill the fish without turning it over. When the fish has flaked easily and reached 145 degrees Fahrenheit, remove from grill.

Nutrition information

This is the nutritional information per 300-calorie serving.

Ø Carbohydrate Servings: 0

À (8) Exchanges: 4 medium-fat meat, 2 fat

LEMON-PEPPER CATFISH

Kale, Sausage, and lentil skillet supper.

Ingredients

1 teaspoon extra virgin olive oil 3 teaspoons of cold pressed olive oil.

"All you need is 12 ounces of chicken sausage." -American Proverb

· 1 large, thin onion slice

·¼ cup chopped garlic

Grated cheese and red pepper on top of the meat.

· 2½ cups water

½ cup of red wine.

·

· Dressed with equal parts Citric Acid and Vitamin C, the Kale easily covers the flavor buds.

You can pour 1 teaspoon of chopped fresh sage over pasta.

· ¼ teaspoon salt

· Freshly ground pepper, to taste.

Preparation

Active: 30 m

Ready In 1:15 min

Why don't you just use the sausages? Okay, heat up a large skillet. Put in a teaspoon of oil. Put in the sausages. .

· Add remaining 2 teaspoons oil to pan and fry the onions and garlic until browned. Add the crushed red pepper and balsamic vinegar and cook until fragrant. Add the water and wine

To the vegetable crispers: sauage, salt and kale.

Nutrition information

½ cup

Ø (pronounced Ø, as in the 'O' in 'obligate') is the recommended serving sizes per day for many different nutrients. For example, the recommended serving of calcium for a man is 320 mg/day. The U. S. Dietary Guidelines tell us that the average man consumes 130 mg per day. The recommended serving size

Ø cereal grains is considered a highly nutritious food by the USDA. Using it, you get a lot of vitamins and minerals.

Carbs: 3 Servings

O

Kale, Rosemary & Sausage Skillet Suppers

COLLARD | GREEN | AND | BLACK-EYED PEA SOUP

Ingredients

· 1 tablespoon extra-virgin olive oil

*A medium sized onion, diced

· 1 large carrot, sliced

1 stalk celery 2-3 cloves garlic, minced 1 Tbsp. oil 1/4 tsp. sea salt 1 Tbsp. fresh oregano,

· 5 cloves of garlic, 4 sliced and 1 whole, divided

A 1/4 cup of chopped fresh thyme Make sure to use synonyms and make key points (not details!) - there are many good substitution words to use.

· ¼ teaspoons crushed red pepper 1/2 teaspoon kosher salt, or to taste In general, we can say paraphrasing requires an

· Reduced-sodium chicken broth

Canned tomatoes (in England)

· 5 cups chopped collard greens or kale

· 1 15-ounce can black-eyed peas, drained

This wonderful bread with its 6½-inch-thick slices, cut on the diagonal, can be a great addition to a variety of dishes.

· · 1 cup shredded cheese

In between the soft, delicate wrapping, you can find a slice of bacon that is hard, thick, and meaty. Actual/Original Video A: Back

Preparation

Active: 45 m

When you are ready in: 45 minutes

In this Italian stew, chopped onion, green pepper, celery and carrot are sauteed in oil before garlic, thyme and crushed red pepper are added. Tomato juice and canned tomatoes are added along with a broth, collard greens (or kale are added and then simmer.

.

To prepare soup topped with cheese toast, place baguette slices on a baking sheet and broil until lightly toasted, two to four minutes. Grate the remaining garlic clove. Top each bread slice with dollops of cheese and broil until the cheese is melted, one to three minutes.

A rimmed baking sheet is great for everything, from roasting to catching accidental drips and spills. To save time and keep your baking sheets in tip-top shape, avoid placing them in regular use by lining them with a layer of foil.

Nutrition information

Eating portions: one-and-a-half cups or one-and-a-half oz

With one teaspoon of soy sauce, the meat was seasoned only a little.

Ø

Ø Carbohydrate Servings: 1½

1 starch, 1 vegetable, ½ medium fat meat, ½ fat

Collard Greens and Black-Eyed Peas

Sink your teeth into a bowl of spicy red beans and rice

Ingredients

¼ cup water

A cup of brown basmati rice. 2½ cups water 2¼ cups vegetable stock/broth/ and can of evaporated skim milk Method: 1.

· ½ teaspoon salt

One tablespoon of extra virgin olive oil.

· 1 cup diced onion

1 15-ounce can red beans, or pink beans, rinsed

· 6 ounces sliced Canadian bacon, chopped

1/2 cup of chopped celery; plus 1 tablespoon of finely chopped celery leaves. ADDITIONAL SUPPORTING ESSAY ACTIVITIES: 1. Two other sections need to be revised. Ask a

· ½ cup diced green bell peppers

As a spice blend, chili powder can be used in a couple of different ways. It can be used as a "heat," much like cayenne, or it can add a little "flavor" to

Preparation

Active: 25 m

5/10 or 50 m

· · ½ cup + 2 Tbs water to make a small amount of porridge. Add rice to a large saucepan, stir in potpourri mixture, then follow the cooking instructions of your previous step.

To prepare the rice, heat the oil. Add the onions and garlic and cook, stirring, until the onions are slightly pink. (A note about Korean cooking: the onions are already cooked when they are added to the rice pot, so there's no need to start the cooking process over from scratch. In this instance the "

· Heat a saucepan on high heat. Add the remaining 1 cup fresh water and bring to a boil. Add the beans, stirring constantly until the beans are crisp-tender, about 5 minutes. Take off the heat, add the Canadian bacon, celery, celery leaves, bell pepper, and the chipotle or cayenne to taste. Serve in shallow bowls and ladle the gravy over the

Chipotles are a type of dried, smoked jalapeño peppers. Ground chipotles can be found in the specialty spice section of most supermarkets, although this ingredient can also be found in other spice sections or

Nutrition information

Ø cup (—)

Ø

Ø A 10 to 20 percent increase in the amount of other vitamins and minerals within a diet is considered a significant increase.

Ø Carbohydrate Servings: 3½

Ð Exchanges: 3 starch, 1 vegetable, 2 lean meat

LOUISIANA RED BEANS & RICE

FRIED GREEN TOMATOES

Ingredients

A mix of cornmeal and yellow cornflour

· Skewers - How-to and tips 1 teaspoon sea salt

Tomatoes are great for digestion. They're a good source of vitamins like C. They're rich in antioxidants.

· Cut the tomatoes into quarters.

· 1 tablespoon extra-virgin olive oil, divided

Preparation

Active: 25 m

Ramp up in: 35 m

The oven needed to be preheated before the food could be put in it to cook.

Grind a medium amount of cornmeal with salt and pepper. Dredge the tomato slices in the mixture.

Brush one and a half teaspoons of oil lightly on the bottom of a neatly-tiled 12-inch ovenproof skillet. Heat the skillet over medium-high heat so that it is glowing hot.

To start, place half the tomatoes on the skillet first, so they brown more and without turning them you transfer the skillet to the oven. Essentially, you're baking seasoned tomatoes instead of simply blanching them. This adds depth to the taste and make additional sauces like salsa, pesto and chipotle sauce better.

· Wipe out skillet and repeat with the remaining 1½ teaspoons of oil and remaining of the tomato slices. Serve hot.

If you have two ovenproof skillets, cook all the tomatoes at the same time.

Nutrition information

The new weight-loss food bar, at a price of $6.64 per serving, contains 64 calories and a blend of soy proteins, brown rice and organic cocoa, and is designed to provide the satiety or fullness of a real meal.

Ø Carbohydrate Servings: ½

Fruits: ½ starch, 1 vegetable, ½ fat

Fried green tomatoes

BRAISED CHICKEN GUMBO

Ingredients

· Stir the olive oil, vinegar and pepper/salt in a bowl.

· a pinch of cayenne and chili powder a medium red or green bell pepper, diced

1 cup all-purpose flour

1 bowl of shredded chicken from Wine & Tomato Braised Chicken (recipe follows)

Napoletana is based on anchovies, olives, capers, and tomatoes.

� cup reduced-sodium chicken broth.

· Use 5-6 cups fresh or frozen okra.

· ¾ cup instant brown rice Tip: · Brown Rice, also called Asian Brown Rice, is

· ⅛- ¼ teaspoon cayenne pepper

Preparation

Active: 20 m

Get ready in 30 minutes

· Crisp your bell pepper and cook the spice mixture until the bell pepper is soft, about 10 minutes. Put the chicken in the saucepan, add the sauce, broth, okra, and rice. Simmer until the flavors meld and the okra is tender, about 10 minutes.

If you're not making this dish from scratch, be sure to use instant rice, or, if you have time, leftover basmati or sticky rice can be added instead. Similarly, if you're not making the dish with the meat, you can substitute 2 cups of leftover chicken, 2 cups of cooked chicken breast, or 3 cups of cooked shrimp instead of the okra.

Nutrition information

1/2 cup

One serving has 347 calories, 15 grams of fat, 3 grams of saturated fat, 3 grams of fiber, 23 grams of carbohydrates, 26 grams of protein, 53 mcg of folate, 78 mg of cholesterol, 4 grams of sugars, zero grams of added sugars, 1,437 IU of vitamin A, 53 mg of vitamin C, 63 mg of calcium

Ø Nutrition Bonus: Vitamin C (88% dv), Vitamin A (29% dv)

Ø Carbohydrate Servings: 1½

Exchange: 1 starch vegetable 3 lean meat 1 fat

BLACK-EYED PEAS WITH GREENS & TOFU

Ingredients

It's best to use two teaspoons of canola oil per pan.

· 1 large onion, sliced Grate the onion over the sink or in a food processor, and squeeze out the juice.

· Dump @11pm 2 pounds pork bacon hock 2 cups onion Paraphrase: Pour the bacon (and removed onions) into a pot.

1 lb of frozen chopped mustard greens or 1 lb of frozen spinach.

· 1 8-ounce package baked, seasoned and smoked tofu, cut into ½-inch dice

4 cups water

· 2 teaspoons hot sauce 3 teaspoons sour cream, plus more to taste ·

1 teaspoon of salt.

·

Preparation

Active: 25 m

Time To Start: 50 m

· Whisk first 7 ingredients in a medium bowl until combined. Add tomato paste and cook, stirring, until very brown. Stir in beef and

For a vegetarian version of this popular recipe, simply substitute vegetable stock for the chicken stock.

Nutrition information

A serving of this salad contains 6 grams of fiber, is a low calorie, and holds trace amounts of vitamins, minerals, and protein.

Ø Dietary Vitamin A (177% dv), Folate (32% dv)

Ø Carbohydrate Servings: 1+

Ø Food exchanges: One starch, one vegetable, one lean meat, one fat.

"BLACK-EYED PEAS WITH GREENS & SMOKED TOFU"

LEMON THINS

Ingredients

1 cup whole-wheat pastry flour is best.

⅓ cup of cornstarch

· · 1½ teaspoons baking powder

3/4 teaspoon salt

butter melted

· 2 tablespoons canola oil

· 1 egg white

My tip is to use freshly grated lemon zest to add personality and a subtle hint of sweetness to it. You can find my other paraphrase tips here and share your ideas

· 1 teaspoon vanilla powder.

· 3 tablespoons lemon juice

Preparation

Active: 30 m

Are you ready in: 45 m?

Form two baking sheets with cooking spray. Spray them thoroughly.

Mix dry ingredients with wet ingredients. Add sugar, butter, oil, egg, and vanilla. Combine ingredients, add juice of ½ lemon, and fold in by hand.

Spoon dough two inches apart on the prepared baking sheet. Use the spoon to drop the dough onto the baking sheet about ¼ cup at a time from a cup measuring 2 inches in diameter. Apply the remaining ¼ cup sugar to a saucer. Dip the bottom of a wide-bottomed glass in the sugar. Using the glass, flatten the dough into a 2½-inch circle. Roll the dough around

· Cook the cookies slowly, and check on them frequently to ensure they are not burning. This should take 8-10 minutes total. Remove to a flat surface (not a rack) to crisp.

Make Ahead Egg Recipe: let's make this a

Nutrition information

1 serving size: 1 cookie

A ITB should (crunch)

½ a cup of carbs

Ø Exchanges: 1 more carb

LEMON THINS

CURRIED SWEET POTATOES

Ingredients

· ·

· 1 teaspoon salt. Plus, more to taste

· ½ cup dried apricots, cut into small pieces

1 cup raisins

· 1 cup boiling water.

· · · · ½ cup cornstarch ½ teaspoon salt ½ cup dark brown sugar 1⁄3 teaspoon cayenne 2 eggs 1 tablespoon water

· To help reduce cancer risk, keep your white blood cells strong. Avoid cancer-causing foods, too.

· · · 3 cups plain yogurt 3 cups milk 4 teaspoons salt First he makes the garlic-yogurt-curry mixture, and it's great,

· Freshly ground pepper, to taste.

Preparation

Active: 35 m

45 Minute Mark Uno

· Place sweet potatoes in a large pot and add enough cold water to cover by 1 inch. Add 1 teaspoon salt and bring to a boil over high heat. Reduce heat to medium and cook, uncovered, until tender but not mushy, 8 to 12 minutes. Drain well.

Meanwhile, combine a few apricots, raisins and a few minutes before, a cup of boiling water in a small bowl; let sit until plump for a few minutes.

To prepare the dish, heat oil in a large, wide, shallow saucepan and sauté the fruit, raisins, and dried apricots. Season with salt and pepper. Stir gently over low heat until warmed through.

Make Ahead Tip: The sweet potatoes can be stored, covered, in the refrigerator for as long as that microwaves can go, usually two hours.

Nutrition information

One serving of the snack has roughly 182 calories and 2 g of fat. It has about 6 g fiber, 41 g carbohydrates, 3 g protein, 11 mg folate, 0 mg cholesterol, 20 g sugars, 0 g added sugar,

24,335 IU vitamin A, 25 mg vitamin C, 63 mg calcium, 1 mg iron, 280 mg sodium, and 8

Concentrated carrots contain several times more energy per serving than carrots eaten as a whole.

Ø 2.5-3 servings of carbohydrates per day

Ø (other carbohydrate sources) - 2½ starch, 1 fruit.

Get a sweet potato and make it CURRIED

JUMPIN' JIMMY'S GUMBO

Ingredients

1 ¼ cup of all-purpose flour. ..... · ⅓ cup all-purpose flour Paraphrase: 1

· 3 teaspoons canola oil.

· 7 oz. boneless, skinless chicken breasts, cut into thin strips

The recipe calls for three ounces of Andouille or kielbasa sausage, thinly sliced.

· 1 Onion.

A large green bell pepper, diced

· 1 stalk of celery then finely chopped

·

· 3 cups reduced sodium chicken broth

· 1 5-minute microwave and 15-second simmer.

· 10-oz. package of frozen okra, slightly thawed, sliced

Scored all over with an ice cube tray.

1 bay leaf

Flash the question on screensaver and play one of the answers. ½ In the fall of 2016, Oreo released a "developmental" version of their Android app.

When you make a mixture of these ingredients, heat about ¼ teaspoon of hot sauce in some of the oil in the pan. Season with salt and pepper.

1 teaspoon salt

· · Salty

· Brown rice Numbe3se 8 cups cooked brown rice

Preparation

Active: 40 m

First toilet in: 1 hour and 15 minutes

To toast flour, heat a skillet over medium heat. Add the flour and stir vigorously with a wooden spoon until the flour is light golden brown. Remove from the heat and transport to a plate to cool.

· Heat a Dutch oven or heavy pot over high heat. Add two teaspoons oil to the Dutch oven and add chicken and sausage. The chicken will brown, and the sausage will poke out meaty bits.

Reduce the heat to medium, and add an additional 1½ teaspoon oil to the pot. Add onion, bell pepper, celery, and garlic. Cook, stirring, until vegetables are tender, about 7 minutes. Stir in the toasted flour, slowly. Stir in broth, and bring to a simmer, stirring.

Add tomatoes and their juice, okra, chiles, bay leaf, and thyme; cover and reduce heat to low. Simmer for 1 hour.

Add the reserved chicken and sausage and simmer for five minutes longer. Discard the chiles and bay leaf. Sauté the chicken and sausage in a pan. Season with hot sauce, salt and pepper. Serve with rice, passing additional hot sauce.

Ingredients: One pound of Andouille sausage, One pound of chicken breasts, Two green onions, 25 chicken bouillon cubes, 25 chicken bouillon bags, One 10 ounce can of creamy chicken soup, One package of the cheese snack, One package of

Nutrition information

a serving size of 400g(about one pound) of cooked spinach contains around 275 calories. It has around 5 grams of fat, 4 grams of fiber, 39 grams of carbohydrates, 17 grams of protein, 140 mcg of folate, 35 mg of cholesterol, 6 grams of sugars, 666 IU of vitamin A, 45 mg of vitamin C

There are a lot of good nutrition bonuses in the food with this superfood status: Vitamin C, Vitamin B6 and Folic P.

Ø Carbohydrates Servings: 2½

The exchange is: 1 white/nut meat, ½ starch, ½ vegetable

Let's go to **JUMPIN' JIMMY'S GUMBO**.

Barbacoa Pork & Coleslaw Sandwiches

Ingredients

Xanthan gum can be used instead of the vinegar.

· 4 teaspoons sugar

Canola oil is an oil derived from the seeds of rapeseed. 2 teaspoons of this oil will be sufficient to cook the recipe.

· 1 tablespoon Dijon mustard

¼ teaspoon celery seeds, ¼ teaspoon ginger ¼ teaspoon apple cider vinegar ¼ teaspoon coriander

Load half a teaspoon of mustard.

· Cabbage salad mix

· ½

· 1 carrot, shredded

Salt & pepper to taste

· 1 teaspoon of canola oil. 2 oval eggs, lightly beaten Paraphrase: Rounded eggs, beaten to a teeter.

If you don't chop one onion, you're not doing it right

· 1 clove garlic, finely chopped 2 teaspoons olive oil a few pinches of salt

1 cup tomato sauce

· Dissolved ¼ cup of vinegar into the water.

· In a small bowl, stir together the maple syrup and brown sugar.

· 1 teaspoon dry mustard. Original: · 1 tablespoon whole mustard seeds Original: ·

Add 1 teaspoon Worcestershire sauce to your food

¼ teaspoon of hot pepper sauce

Salt to taste

2 pork tenderloins might be trimmed of fat and opened up.

2 or, in a pinch, 4. ....1 Kaiser or other large roll, split ....1 Kaiser or other large roll, split ....12 Kaiser or other large

Preparation

Active: 40 m

Go in: 40 m

This is how to make coleslaw: Whisk together vinegar, sugar, oil, Dijon mustard, celery seeds, and mustard seeds. Add cabbage and carrots, and stir well. Season with salt and pepper.

To make barbecue sauce, rub pureed onions and garlic with ketchup, adding spices and other ingredients. Heat the sauce and boil until boiling point.

Cook the pork on the grill, placing the meat on a hot grill and grilling until the internal temperature reaches 160°F, about 5 minutes. Here is the process. First, season the meat with salt and pepper. Next, broil it on a barbecue grill over the highest heat setting so the meat browns nicely. While the pork broils in the oven, make barbecue sauce by blending all the ingredients together.

Put a burger on bread, then top it with coleslaw and sliced pork.

Nutrition information

Based on per capita consumption of all foods approximate per capita food supply of all foods. I realized how long it took to make coffee. 1 hour and 12 minutes. I finally got my hands back on the coffee maker.

Her daily diet consisted of 42% of vitamin A, 25% of vitamin C.

- Carbohydrate Servings: 4

A phrase would be 1 starch 2 other carbohydrate 3½ lean meat

Barbecued pork & coleslaw sandwiches

BARBECUE CHICKEN KALE WRAPS

Ingredients

· 8 kale leaves, or four large, cut in half crosswise

Use one tablespoon canola oil.

· 1 pound boneless, skinless chicken breast, trimmed and cut into bite-size pieces.

· ¼teaspoonsalt

Approximately 5 tablespoons

1 tablespoon

½ teaspoon cajun seasoning.

· 1 cup thinly sliced red cabbage

.... 2 cups carrots 1 cup julienned carrots Paraphrase: ....

A 1/4 cup minced scallion and a chopped wedge of fresh greens (arugula, spinach, watercress or other green).

Preparation

Active: 30 m

Ready in: 30 minutes

· How to clean your kale leaves.

Make sure the oil is hot in a large, nonstick skillet. Add the chicken and season it with salt. Stir with a spoon to coat everything with oil. Let it cook until the meat is almost done, 4 or six minutes.

· Meanwhile, make a barbecue sauce by combining ketchup, soy sauce, vinegar, and Cajun seasonings in a small bowl.

Place the sauce in the stock pot and heat the sauce. Serve the sauce in the cabbage leaves, over a pile of roasted carrots and topped with scallion greens.

Nutrition information

Ø Serving size: Two wraps

kcal (calories) - 181 carbohydrates - 7 g fat - 24 g protein - 15 g sugar - 3 g fiber - 2 g cholesterol - 69 mg sodium - 9 g potassium - 498 mg iron - 7 mg vitamin A - 913 IU vitamin C -

The levels of vitamin A

Ø Carbohydrate Servings: 1

Omelette, ½ other carbohydrate, 1 vegetable, 3 lean meat, ½ fat

BURGER CHICKEN CHEESE KALE WRAPS

,

Ingredients

. 1 pound red or yellow potatoes, cut into

· 4 cups chopped kale, stems removed.

1/2 cup avocado or canola oil

· two tablespoons of ground chili powder

1/2 teaspoon paprika

Add ½ teaspoon salt to the sauce.

½ teaspoon garlic powder

· 2 8- to 10-ounce boneless pork chops, about �

4 tablespoons of processed meat

2 tablespoons of water

Preparation

Active: 40 m

40 minutes

.

· Lay the potato and kale mixture in the center of the foil. Coat with oil, chili powder, paprika, salt and garlic powder. Wrap tightly, weaving the foil shut with twine. Wrap the potato and kale mess in the center of a foil packet. Bake the stuffed potato and kale for 25 minutes, or until the potatoes are tender.

· Meanwhile, heat the remaining oil in a skillet. Sprinkle pork with salt. Cook, turning once, until an instant-read thermometer inserted into the center registers 145 degrees Fahrenheit. Transfer pork to a clean cutting board. Cut into slabs.

Combine 3/4 cup barbecue sauce with 1/4 cup water in a large sauce pan. Add the pork, turning to coat with the sauce. Serve the kale and potatoes with the pork, drizzled with any sauce remaining in the pan.

Nutrition information

They had 12 oz. i.e. 2 slices of bread with 2 tbsp. ham, a slice of cheese and 1 cup salad.

** One serving is approximately 364 calories (or one medium-size sweet potato or one apple).

"Vo is a vegetable rich in Vitamin C and vitamins A and E. The daily consumption of these vegetables in the form of salad can significantly contribute to the overall health."

Ø Carbohydrate Servings: 2½

Percentages and dietary exchanges

bARBECUED PORK CHOPS WITH ROASTED POTATOES & KALE

TURKEY SHRIMP, PECORINO OATMEAL (PER SERVING)

Ingredients

6 tablespoons of extra-virgin olive oil. A: The original one is a bit too complex to be shortened substantially... Is it possible to paraphrase '

3 teaspoons of butter in half serving size.

You . You chopped the scallions into scallions. 7 English peas, frozen shelled Paraphrase: You boiled the English peas.

Oat flour is a wonderful alternative to bread, these are nutritious and taste great. 1 cup old-fashioned rolled oats

available water

Take 1 teaspoon salt and 2/3 teaspoon table salt.

A pinch of pepper.

· 1 pound raw shrimp (16-20 count; see Tip), peeled, deveined, and tails

⅛ teacup cayenne pepper, or to taste

· 1 pound baby spinach

SEVEN of your favorite toppings to put on Seven.

· A half cup of grated Pecorino or Parmesan cheese.

Preparation

Active: 30 m

Be ready in: 30 m

Add the scallion whites, oats, salt, and pepper to a medium batch pan and cook, stirring often, for several minutes to heat through and get going. Add water and a few tablespoons and bring to a boil. Reduce heat to a simmer and cook for many minutes until creamy and the oats are cooked through.

Meanwhile, in a large frying pan, sprinkle shrimp with pepper, add cayenne and 1 tablespoon oil and saute until the shrimp turn opaque, about 2 to 4 minutes per side. Transfer to a clean bowl and cover to keep warm.

Take a pan. Add 1 teaspoon of oil. Add half of the spinach. Cook and stir until slightly wilted, about one minute. Then add the remaining spinach. Cook and stir until wilted, two to three minutes more. Add hot sauce. Leave salt out.

Mix cheese and butter into the oats, then add the spinach and shrimp. Sprinkle with scallion greens.

Choose sustainably-raised shrimp. Look for shrimp that are Martin certified. If you cannot find Martin certified shrimp, choose Atlantic Northwest wild-caught shrimp.

Celiac disease sufferers should use gluten-free oats to avoid cross-contamination and contamination.

Nutrition information

·

The following is an A DAY IN THE LIFE of a man of about 50 years of age. The measurements are expressed per servings.

Calcium

· Carbohydrate Servings: 1½

It's important to: Make sure you choose whole grains. Cut down on other foods with refined carbohydrates, like bread, pasta, and rice. Include more vegetables and lean meats, but also choose more fat-

TWO-PEPPER SHRIMP WITH CREAMY PECORINO OAT

SWEET MEATLOAF

Ingredients

· 1½ pounds collard greens (approximately 2 bunches)

· 2 tablespoons extra-virgin olive oil

· 1 onion, diced

· 3 cloves of minced garlic.

-1 teaspoon kosher salt, divided

Start with two tablespoons of hot sauce.

1/2 teaspoon Worcestershire sauce

·

· ½ teaspoon smoked paprika

A teaspoon of pepper helps to clear the sinuses.

A cup remains a cup and the equivalent of 1 cup if each breadcrumb is fine. Using a tablespoon will give you 1½ cups of crumbs. Pasting: In another bowl

Butter | Reduced-fat milk

· 1 pound 90%-lean ground beef or bison

· 1 pound nutritious ground pork

I poured a large bowl of fluffy scrambled eggs: two large, lightly beaten eggs.

¾ cup ketchup and ¼ cup water.

Preparation

Active: 45 m

Room for: 2 h

· Cut up a bunch of collard greens.

When collard greens are wilted, they are ready to serve as a side dish. Add hot sauce and seasonings to taste and stir well to incorporate the ingredients. Note: Hot sauce is optional; you can substitute your favorite dipping sauce.

Soak bread in milk to create the breadcrumb. Once the bread has soaked, add in nuts and cheese.

· · Meanwhile, coat a large rimmed baking sheet with cooking spray (see tip, below).

· Add meat (or bison) to the greens, eggs (we used a hard boiled egg for our recipe), ½ cup of ketchup, 1 breadcrumb, and 1 teaspoon salt, then gently mix by hand to combine. Cut into four or six slices to fit your individual loaf pans. Bake until the internal temperature of the bread is

· For 30 minutes, brush the top with the remaining ¼ cup ketchup.

· Once the oven has heated up to 400 degrees, increase the temperature to that of the middle oven rack. Continue to bake the bread until a thermometer inserted into the center registers 165 degrees Fahrenheit, 25 to 35 minutes. Set the bread aside after

A cook doesn't have to clean sticky spray residue from the baking sheet. Just after spraying the item with the cooking spray, lay a sheet of aluminum foil over it.

Nutrition information

One serving is roughly a slice (half-an-inch)

For every meal, you should get 2/3 cup cooked beans and some kind of vegetables every day and also have a little bit of meat though not more than 100 grams. Therefore, you must add 3 servings of cooked beans per day and eat a smaller amount of meat.

Add this list to your running routine for a healthy boost: vitamin A, vitamin C, folate, and calcium.

Starch exchanges including ½ starch, ½ vegetable and 1 other carbohydrate, 3 lean meat and ½ fruits, ½ medium-fat meat and ½ fat.

SPICY MEATLOAF WITH COLLARDS

SOUTHERN BEETS & GREENS WITH CHEVRE SPOONBREAD

Ingredients

Spoonbread

½ cup reduced-fat milk. Like milk, my body needs calcium to produce strong bones.

Eat 1 teaspoon of sugar

¾ teaspoon kosher salt.

· ¼ teaspoon cayenne pepper

¾ cup of cornmeal

· 3 tablespoons unsalted butter, room temperature, cut into small pieces

3 eggs, at room temperature, separated.

· · · (With a light hand) (using larger cheese and a drier hand) ¾ cup crumbled soft goat cheese

Mix spinach and beets

· four medium beets

Eat 2 medium oranges

Put a quarter cup of red-wine vinegar in a pot; heat it up to a simmer.

· honey

· 1/2 to ¼ teaspoon crushed red pepper

· Salt ¼ teaspoon + the salt

· 1 tablespoon cold unsalted butter

· In a small saucepan, cook chopped beet greens or chard stems in 3 1/2 cups of water.

· 2 Tbsp olive oil. The "(blank)" in the original sentence indicates the paragraph should be

· · · · · · 3 cloves of garlic long sliced

White wine is a good accompaniment to this fish dish.

· Unevenly sprinkled with kosher salt.

Preparation

Active: 1 h

One Hour

·

Steam the beets. Make sure to cook them covered, avoiding any excessive steaming. Once cooked, slice the beets into half-inch thick wedges.

To prepare spooncakes, layer the cream and pudding into the prepared baking dish in alternate layers. After the pudding has set, spoon a ball of the pudding on top and spread. Use a glass or mason jar to spread the pudding around the outside of the dish. Place in a pre-heated oven at 375°F and bake until cooked through, about 30 minutes. Place a piece of spoonbread, cooked side down, on a plate

Whisk egg yolks and the remaining half cup of milk in a large bowl until well combined. Add goat cheese and whisk until incorporated.

Beat eggs with an electric mixer in a medium mixing bowl until soft peaks form. Blend one third of the cornmeal mixture into the yolk mixture. Gently flip the batter and fold in the remaining cornmeal mixture. Swirl the batter in another bowl to lighten the consistency. Pour the batter into the prepared baking dish. 2. Bake at 425°F for about 15 minutes, or until the cake is set. Place

Bake the spoonbread until puffed and golden, but still damp in the center.

· What you'll need: · · 1/2 cup fresh orange juice 1/2 cup ketchup 1 tablespoon honey 1 tablespoon red pepper flakes salt • Reserve 1 cup of the orange juice for the roasting and glazing method. Directions: • Preheat oven to 350F. • Strip the zest from

Use a large, heavy pan like a skillet, and heat oil in it. Add garlic and mix in beet greens stems. Add the greens to the pan and season with wine, salt and pepper. Cook greens, stirring frequently, about 5 minutes.

· At the table, serve the beets and greens with the warm spoonbread.

Please prepare the beets by boiling or steaming. You can store beets and reheat them in the oven later.

Nutrition information All the "nutrition information"

1/2cup of cooked pasta 1 tablespoon of sun-dried tomatoes 1/2 cup of steamed broccoli 12 small asparagus spears salt and pepper to taste Combine all dry ingredients together. In a bowl, combine tomato sauce with water as you would for sauce as you would for sauce as you would for a normal

Ø Risks (62% dv)

Ø Carbohydrate Servings: 2

bread, grains, cereal, fat-free milk, meat, and fat

SOUTHERN BEETS & CHEVRE!

CREAMED KALE

Ingredients

2 tablespoons extra-virgin olive oil.

· 1½ cups sliced leek, all white and light green parts.

·

· 2 cloves of garlic, finely minced

¾ teaspoon salt

· ½ teaspoon sweet paprika

Add ¼-¾ cups of water, as needed.

2 tablespoons all-purpose flour

1 cup of skim. 2 cups reduced-fat milk Paraphrase: 2 cups of skim.

This is a wonderful dish. It's full of flavor and also healthy. It's great if you like nutmeg.

Preparation

Active: 30 m

You're ready in 30 minutes

Cook asparagus, leek, mushrooms, and garlic together. Cook until the asparagus is soft. Sprinkle the greens with flour, stir in milk, and cinnamon and nutmeg (if using).

Cut the thick white part of the leek in rounds and rinse in plenty of water until no grit remains.

Nutrition information

·

For a mere 109 calories, you can experience all of the vitamins, herbs, and minerals listed above by using this product.

· Foods to eat so that you can get the vitamins you need.

· Carbohydrate Servings: ½

· Exchange: 3 vegetables, 1 fat

CREAMED KALE

THE GOOD FARMER COCKTAIL

Ingredients

· A sprig of mint

· Crushed ice

1.3 cups of lemonade (6.2 ounces). ¼ cup sugar (2.4 ounces) Paraphrase: ⅓ cup sugar (1.2

He poured bourbon into his glass and downed it in one go.

· Lemon slice for garnish

Preparation

Active: 5 m

How To Get Ready: 5 minutes

Adding fresh mint to a pint glass containing crushed ice and lemonade. This popular trend must be followed carefully, lest you find yourself with a mint-ade cocktail instead of a Whipper-In Pimm's cocktail.

Nutrition information

Ø Serving size: 8 ounces

Per 8-gram serving, this snack contains 2.1 servings of grains, 2.1 of protein, 0.1 of dietary fiber, 4.8 grams of carbohydrates, 0 grams of fat, 0 milligrams of vitamin A, 0 milligrams of vitamin C, 237 milligrams of calcium, 0 milligrams of iron, 226 mill

½ carbohydrate serving

1 other carbohydrate, 2 fat

THE GOOD FARMER

Ingredients

· 2 medium kohlrabi (about 1 1/2 pounds), peeled

· 2 medium carrots

The baby had a small head, but it radicchio.

The cider vinegar fixes, the beet purges and the orange juice rids - it will help to build a healthy and beautiful body

· 3 teaspoons honey

· teaspoon of Dijon mustard · 2 cartons of low-fat milk · · 1 tablespoon monoglyceride · · 1 tablespoon lecithin ·

¼ teaspoon celery seeds

½ teaspoon salt

.. ground itself was pepper.

Oranges, apples, and honey

¼ cup roasted unsalted sunflower seeds

Preparation

Active: 15 m

In: 15 minutes Original: Test yourself. Paraphrase: Measure yourself. Original: Full Body Workout Paraphrase

· Combine kohlrabi, carrots and radicchio in a large bowl.

· Even though it's a combination of ingredients found in many commercial salad dressings, it's a dish that you may never find in the large city supermarkets where most people get their vegetables.

· The bowl is filled with the combination of kohlrabi, carrots, radicchio, and sauerkraut. Sprinkle with sunflower seeds. Wordiness: If you have trouble coming up with

If you want to enjoy sunflower seeds later, make them ahead. Refrigerate them in an airtight container for up to 2 hours; top each cup with seeds just before serving.

When serving salads, add nuts, raisins, or seeds right before they're served so they don't get soggy.

Nutrition information

Already 2 hours of exercise?

Ø Nutrition

Ø Carbohydrate Servings: 1

½ other carbohydrate, 1 vegetable, 1½ fat

Honey Kohlrabi Slaw with Radicchio

I'm hungry; brb

Ingredients

1 large box of whole-wheat elbow noodles (6-8 cups)

· 2 cups chopped collard greens 2 tablespoons fat free powdered milk 2 tablespoons chickpea flour (besan)

½ cup skim milk ½ cup whole milk

· 3 tablespoons all-purpose flour · 3 tablespoons all-purpose flour

· ¼ teaspoon salt

One-fourth teaspoon of pepper.

1 cup shredded extra sharp Cheddar cheese

Counts of 2 grams of fat.

· 2 teaspoons of white-wine vinegar

· ¼ cup unseasoned whole-wheat breadcrumbs, preferably made from scratch

·

· ½ teaspoon powder seasoning

Preparation

Active: 30 m

Ready in: 30 minutes

· Wash the collards and cut off the bottoms and heat two large pots of water. Add pasta and cook according to the pasta package directions. Drain.

1. Pull from the refrigerator and transfer to a heat proof bowl. 2.Meanwhile whisk together to yolks with remaining milk in a medium bowl until frothy. 3. Whisk in the Cheddar cheese and the cream cheese and until the cheese is melted. 4. Add the vinegar and whisk in the rice flour until combined. 5. Whisk in the milk mixture until incorporated.

· Preheat the broiler to high.

· Add breadcrumbs, oil and paprika to the pasta {the pasta's water} and hill the pasta until it comes to a boil. Quickly remove from the heat and toss with the topping until evenly coated. Serve immediately.

Nutrition information

a serving size: about 1⅔ cups

According to the Dietary Guidelines for Americans, the average adult should have up to two 4-ounce servings of low-fat or nonfat milk per day. One serving is 180 calories with 16 grams of fat. Just 70 calories and 2 grams of fat are found in one cup with skim milk.

A diet high in vitamin A, calcium, and vitamin C may help protect against the symptoms of zinc deficiency and help support healthy growth and development.

Four portions of carbohydrates per day

Lunch consisted of a breadstick, 3 starch (potato, pasta, rice) meals and a high-fat meat, pasta, rice meal!

The **MAC & CHEESE** is quite filling and good!

BBQ PULLED CHICKEN SANDWICH WITH COLES

Ingredients

· 1 pound, boneless, skinless, chicken breast, trimmed

Two and one-half cups of vinegar

So, you're adding 2 tablespoons sugar to ________.½ cup of warm water.

· (½ teaspoon) is a pepper. This is (½ teaspoon) a pepper. This is Degree of Education: Adult

½ teaspoon Cayenne Pepper ______

· 1/4 cup salt, divided

¾ cup buttermilk

½ cup reduced-fat mayo ·

· ½ tsp celery seed ½ tsp celery seed ½ tsp celery seed

½ teaspoon ground pepper

·

· · 4 small soft brown rolls, heated if desired

Preparation

Active: 30 m

Ready In: 40 m

1. Choose a medium skillet to prepare a chicken. 2. Fill a medium saucepan 1/2 inch with water. 3. Bring to a boil. 4. Reduce heat and simmer gently. 5. Slow Cook Chicken

· Meanwhile, combine vinegar, 1 tablespoon of sugar, crushed red pepper and cayenne in a large bowl over medium heat. Reduce the heat to medium-low, and cook for 8 minute. Take off the heat. Stir in a ¼ teaspoon of salt. Preserve the pan over an ice bath. When the sauce has

· Use two forks to shred chicken into bite-size pieces. Stir the chicken into the sauce until well combined. Cover and let marinate for 10 minutes.

Add the remaining sugar, salt, and buttermilk to the cream cheese. Add the celery and pepper and mix. Then add the coleslaw and toss to combine. Serve the chicken on buns (or rolls) with the slaw and any extra cream cheese on the side.

Nutrition information

A serving of chicken is ⅔ cup. A bun and 1 cup of slaw are added to this amount.

Here's a tip for how to eat a lot without gaining weight: Decrease the number of calories you consume PER SERVING by more than half. This way, you'll actually consume 40% fewer calories than if you ate the same food, but with twice as many servings. #genius #paraphrase #dictionary

Children often lack the basic nutrients found in produce, such as vitamin A, vitamin C, folate.

2 Carb Servings

Ø Exchanges: 1 starch (cooked rice, bread, pasta), 1½ vegetable (1 eggplant and 1 carrot), ½ other carbohydrate (1 egg), 3½ lean meat (

Build a sandwich for yourself

OVEN-FRIED GREEN TOMATILLOS

Ingredients

· Canola oil spraying equipment

· 1 pound tomatillos (about 12 medium), peeled and cut into 1/2- to 1-inch-thick slices

1 teaspoon salt

· Use **splash** of **ketchup and vinegar** for the next "gourmet" food.

½ cup flour with ¼ cup water mixed into it.

A teaspoon of garlic powder. 2 teaspoons of ground mustard Paraphrase: Two teaspoons of ground mustard. 10 qu

· 1 teaspoon Creole or Cajun seasoning

·

English muffins · 1 teaspoon Dijon mustard For the topping· 1 tablespoon may

· 1 teaspoon ketchup

Preparation

Active: 35 m

Ready In: 35 m

· Position a rack in lower third of oven; preheat to 425°F. Coat a large baking sheet with cooking spray.

Pre-heat oven grill to high. Pour off any juice from the canned tomatillos. Combine the flour, garlic powder, Creole (or Cajun) seasoning and salt and pepper in a shallow dish. Mix the eggs in a separate dish vigorously but evenly until foamy. Dip the tomatillos into the floured flour mixture, dip into the egg, then coat with breadcrumbs

· Bake the tomatillos, rotating them once about halfway through the cooking time.

I've created a dipping sauce out of mayonnaise and ketchup. I recommend using it on any tomatillos sauced with my sauce.

To reduce the time and effort involved in cleaning the sheet, spray it first before lining it with foil.

Nutrition information

Serve yourself a small portion of tomato slices and sauce.

One serving of Original Crispbread contains 131 calories, 4 grams of fat, 2 servings of fiber, 0 grams of carbohydrates, 3 grams of protein, 0.5 mcg of folate, 23 milligrams of cholesterol, 6 grams of sugars, 2 grams of added sugars, 19 milligrams of Vitamin A, 9 milligrams of Vitamin C,

1½ glass of Carbohydrate Servings

You should eat ø exchanges: 1 starch, 1 vegetable, ½ fat

OVEN-FRIED TOMATILLOS

BACON-WRAPPED PORK CHOPS SMOTHERED WITH THICK BOURBON GLAZE AND HOP

Ingredients

· 4 tablespoons molasses

Cinnamon can be used to add a subtle flavor to drinks.

· 1 tablespoon Dijon mustard

4 bone-in pork chops (¼- ½ inch thick; about 2 pounds), trimmed

· ¾ teaspoon of salt, divided

Equal to ¾-teaspoon of ground pepper.

1½ tablespoons extra-virgin olive oil · ½ teaspoon salt

1 medium sized green bell pepper, diced

· 1 large onion, chopped 2 cloves garlic, minced 1.5 Tbsp each butter & olive

3 cloves of garlic, minced

· 1 15-ounce can black-eyed peas-rinsed

· ¾ teaspoon smoked paprika A: I have had to write a similar email and I

½ teaspoon of dried thyme, ·

Preparation

Active: 45 m

Get in: 45 m

Combine molasses, apple juice and mustard and season pork chops with half of a teaspoon each salt and pepper. Brush each pork chop with half of the molasses glaze.

· Position rack in upper third of oven; preheat broiler to high.

· Heat 1 tablespoon oil in a large cast-iron or other broiler-safe skillet over medium-high heat. Add the pork chops and cook until golden brown, 2 to 3 minutes per side. Transfer to a plate.

Put the remaining oil in a heavy skillet. Add the peppers, onion, and garlic. Stir and cook until the vegetables are soft. Add the black-eyed peas, paprika, thyme, and seasonings. Add the pork chops. Pour in any accumulated juices from the pork. Brush the pork chops with additional glaze. Put the pan under the broiler. Cook until the meat is tender, 2 to 5 minutes, depending on the thickness of the chops.

Nutrition information

Serving size: 1 chop, 55ml and 1 cup Hoppin' John (calculated from recipe)

This afternoon I managed to measure the vegetarian cheese spread's per-serving calorific value and found it to be around 400 calories. 6. Metaphors 4. Supersize Me

Ø 65% daily value of Vitamin C

Ø Carbohydrate Servings: 1½

I'll have ½ starch, 5 lean meats, and 1½ fats.

Pork chops glazed in bourbon and served with Hopin' John

PIMIENTO-CHEESE PATTY MELT

Ingredients

½ cup grated onion ¾ cup grated cheese (sharp is best)

1 tablespoon Worcestershire sauce

· 1 teaspoon paprika

·~½ teaspoon garlic powder

¼ teaspoon salt

· ¼ tsp freshly cracked pepper

1lb lean ground beef 2 eggs

Scatter small cubes of sharp cheese over the top of the omelet.

· 2 tablespoons reduced-fat mayonnaise

· Chopped in a deep pan, two tablespoons of jarred pimientos can be added to the dish.

2 tablespoons chopped spring onions

Instead of toast, you could have: ·4 slices whole wheat country bread · 4 teaspoons sugar · 6 tablespoons trans fat-free margarine

Preparation

Active: 30 m

Ready in: 30 minutes

Combine onion, Worcestershire, paprika, garlic powder, salt and pepper in a medium bowl. Then combine the ground beef with the other ingredients. Remove any visible fat. Form into 4 burgers, about the same size as the bread you're using.

· Coat a large nonstick skillet with cooking spray and set over medium-high heat. Add the burgers and cook, turning once, until just cooked through, 8 to 10 minutes total.

On the side, stir together the cheese, mayonnaise, diced pimientos, and diced scallions.

· Place toast on a baking sheet. Top each piece with a burger and about 2 tablespoons of the cheese mixture. Broil until the cheese starts to brown, about 2 minutes.

Get a rimmed baking sheet: It will help a lot at cleanup and to keep your baking sheets from getting bent.

Nutrition information

Ø one patty melt: 12"

Ø Per serving: 336 cal; 15g fat(6.5g sat); 2g fiber; 17g carbs; 29.4g protein; 27 mcg folate; 88 mcg cholesterol; 4 g sugars; 2 g.

Ø Nutrition Bonus: Iron (22% daily value)

Most Americans have less than the recommended maximum of 40 grams of carbohydrate per day in their diet. In fact, many people limit themselves to as little as 25 grams per day.

Be sure to have bread, starches, and meat in your diet. Also, eat vegetables, lean meats, and fats.

Peanut butter and banana patty melt

BOURBON WHIPPED CREAM

Ingredients

1 cup heavy cream 1 cup heavy cream.

· 3 tablespoons confectioners' sugar

1 tablespoon of bourbon

"·" is 1 tablespoon vanilla.

Preparation

Active: 5 m

5 m Ready In

· After whisking the cream with sugar in the bowl using the mixer, add the bourbon and vanilla and continue to beat until stiff peaks form.

Nutrition information

O Serving size: 1 tbsp.

10 teaspoons of granola which has 30 calories and 3 grams of fat contain about one percent of the potassium that's required by the human body.

Serve no carbs

Eat: ½ fats, ½ carbs

Be the best you that you can be.

APPLE BOURBON GRAVY

Ingredients

1 tablespoon of olive oil.

1/3 cup chopped onion

¼ cup celery chopped.

½ cup chopped carrot

· ¾ cup bourbon

·

How many people use the computer, tablet or smartphone?

· A cup of apple cider

¼ cup water ¼ cup milk ¼ cup coffee ¼ cup black tea ¼ cup orange juice ¼ cup lemon juice ¼

3 tablespoons all-purpose flour.

4 tablespoons of unsalted butter is best cut into 8 pieces.

· 1/8 teaspoon salt

Preparation

Active: 30 m

Complete in 1 hour and 15 minutes

Add the shallots, celery and carrot to a large saucepan. Pour in the bourbon. Increase heat to medium-high and cook until the bourbon is mostly evaporated, about 3 minutes. Add the thyme.

Adding chicken broth and 1 cup of cider to your simmering pot of soup reduces the base by almost half in about an hour.

In the meantime, mix water and flour in a small bowl.

In this recipe, a roux is made by adding a small amount of shortening or butter to a large amount of flour. This combination is whisked in a pan until a paste is formed, which we know as a breading. It's then added to the casserole and drizzled with butter. Make sure to add the grease in small amounts. If there is too much fat, the roux will become

My advice: Make ahead tip: Cover and refrigerate for up to 3 days. Reheat and serve before 4 p.m. to save the most time.

Nutrition information

Ø Serving size: ¼-cup

A serving of this product totals 110 calories, 5 grams of fat, 0 grams of fiber, 7 grams of carbs, 2 grams of protein,15 mg of folate, 10 mg of cholesterol, 3 grams of sugar, 0 grams of added sugar, 1,602 IU of vitamin A, 2 mg of vitamin C, 11 mg of calcium,

Ø (vitamin A (32% daily value))

Ø Carbohydrate Servings: ½

½ vegetable, 1 fat.

APPLE BOURBON GREMOLATA

SWEET &

Ingredients

· 2 teaspoons chili powder

· 4 teaspoons of brown sugar

Mustard tastes good? The Ground Cumin looks kind of dirty. How about the Delta Mustard? · 2 plum tomatoes Paraph

·¼ teaspoon salt

· ½a teaspoon smoked paprika

The bowl of "Nemo's Cajun salt and pepper mix" provided a nice base of seasonings for the fish to stand on.

My mom uses ginger for a cough syrup. From the original cheatsheet A: The original document has 2 sections: Mis/disinformation and

1/4 teaspoon cayenne pepper

Preparation

Active: 5 m

You can be ready in 15 minutes.

· Combine chili powder, brown sugar, cumin, salt, paprika, garlic powder, ginger and cayenne in a small bowl.

Nutrition information

Prepare your meal by putting the ingredients in bowls and measuring with a teaspoon

As for calories, it has zero

Ø 1/2 Carb Servings

Sweet & Spicy BBQ Rub 2- 10 minutes

HERBED CORNBREAD STUFFING

Ingredients

Cornbread

1½ cups cornmeal

· 1 cup all-purpose flour

3 tablespoons of sugar

· ½ t.

⅛ teaspoon salt

· You'll need 1 cup of buttermilk to make this frosting.

· ½ cup skim milk

· St. Louis-style Italian crepe

1 cup of cold water

...melted butter.

· Oil

Stuffing

1 stick of unsalted butter ||

¼ cup chopped Celery Original: · ½ cup chopped onion Paraphrase: ½ cup chopped Onion Original: ½ cup corn

· 1 cup big onions

A 2-inch-thick circle was a match for the thick and juicy apples. I chopped them into quarters, then quarters into chunks. I liked the two-step process of peeling then chopping

.

· 1½ tablespoons finely chopped fresh thyme.

½ cup reduced-sodium chicken stock; or, ½ cup reduced-sodium chicken broth

· 3 tablespoons finely-chopped flat-leaf parsley.

· Old Bay Seasoning

¼ teaspoon

· Add a pinch of ground black pepper to add a little variety to your spice cup.

Preparation

Active: 50 m

Ready in 2 hours.

Mix cornmeal-based dough.

A department store in southeastern Michigan was fined $7,000 after an employee admitted to stealing more than $1,700 in merchandise. However, they only wanted to be fired and had no intention of returning the money. But he was was wearing a wire and turned up the goods.

· Spread the dough into the prepared pan and bake until a toothpick in the center comes out clean, about 25 to 30 minutes. Let cool completely on a wire rack. The dough needs to be partially cooled to avoid it becoming too sticky as it is stuffed. If it becomes too sticky,

.

· In a large skillet, melt the butter. Add the apples and vegetables and cook, stirring occasionally, until softened, about 8 to 10 minutes.

Meanwhile, combine crumbled cornbread into a large bowl.

In a bowl, add ½ cup of the cornbread mix to the pumpkin filling. Mix well.

• Melt the remaining butter and add to the stuffing mixture along with parsley, Old Bay, salt and pepper. Combine the stuffing mixture with the prepared dish and cover tightly with foil.

Cook the stuffing for 30 minutes. Take the foil off and continue baking, until slightly browned, another 20 to 25 minutes.

Make Ahead: Make cornbread (Steps 1 to 3). Prepare stuffing through Step 8, cover and refrigerate for up to 1 day. Remove from the refrigerator about thirty minutes before you bake the bread.

Nutrition information

Heaping ½ cup

Ø

Ø Carbohydrate Servings: 2

One and a half carbs, half veggies, three fats for a good day.

Stuff the Cornbread with a herb mix

All American BBQ chicken breast on a buttery dill biscuit

Ingredients

½ cup ketchup

A suitable amount of beer. A porter

· Sugar: ½ cup molasses ½ cup molasses, when added to water, causes it to boil faster. Similarly, if you have spent your life on a diet

→ 2 tablespoons of juice

Two tablespoons of cider vinegar.

·

· ·

Cook onions and onion powder in butter and add salt and pepper.

· 2 **tablespoons** hot sauce, or to taste

· 4 (8-ounce) boneless, skinless chicken breasts, trimmed

·

· 1/3 cup salt

¼ teaspoon freshly ground pepper

Preparation

Active: 30 m

Ready In: Less than 50 m

Combine the following in a medium heavy saucepan and simmer, stirring frequently: ketchup; beer; molasses; orange juice; vinegar; mustard and onion powder. Reduce heat to maintain a simmer; cook, stirring frequently, until reduced to about 1½ cups, 20 to 25 minutes; then stir in hot sauce.

Smith needed to grill the chicken so that it was cooked. He placed the meat on a flat grill griddle and turned it on. When the underside looked grilled, he moved the meat to the other side.

Place chicken breasts halves in a medium bowl and coat with oil. Season with salt and pepper.

Heat a stove-top grill, brush with some barbecue sauce, and cook the chicken, with the lid closed, until lightly browned. Turn the chicken and brush with another sauce, close the lid and cook until an instant-read thermometer in the thickest part of the chicken registers 165°F. Serve with more barbecue sauce on the side, if desired. Next, set up your poster again and draw a line on each side of the box. Label the left side of the box "Enforcement" and the right side of the box, "Protect & Provide."

Cover any leftover sauce, refrigerate, and use within 1 week.

Rub the grill to make sure the grill is well preheated. Then, blot it with a folded paper towel before placing the chicken on the grill.

Nutrition information

Ø = olive Serving size: 3 oz. chicken & 1 Tbsp sauce

(servings = approximately 0.33) For one serving, 219 calories are derived from carbohydrates, protein, fats, and sodium; 13 g of added sugars are in the natural sugars from the fruit; there is 3 mg of vitamin C from the fruit, plus trace amounts from the source, and 2 mg of iron.

Ø Carbohydrate Servings: 1

Ø

All-American BBQ Chicken Breast

BLACK-EYED PEA DIP

Ingredients

· A 16-ounce can of black-eyed peas.

· 2 tablespoons extra-virgin olive oil

Here are the simple steps to making a home-cooked rice dish:

· Mince the garlic.

· 1 teaspoon dried thyme rub.

... until he added another tablespoon and some more to his food.

Preparation

Active: 10 m

Ready In: 10 minutes: Combine black-eyed peas, oil, vinegar, garlic, thyme, and hot sauce in a blender. Puree until smooth.

Nutrition information

Ø teaspoon: 1 tablespoon

Ø per serving: 24 calories; 1 g fat; 1 g fiber; 2 g carbohydrate; 1 g protein; 8 mcg of folate; 0 mg of cholesterol; /g sugars; 4 IU of vitamin A; 0 mg of vitamin C; 4 mg of calcium; 0 mg of iron; 30 mg of sodium;

0 carbohydrate servings

Ø Exchanges: free lunch

Black-Eyed Peas Dip

ALL-AMERICAN BBQ SAUCE

Ingredients

3/4 cup ketchup

A man has a thirst for beer, preferably porter. This how to paraphrase tutorial is the fastest and easiest way to learn what paraphrasing is and how to

· ½ cup molasses

1 cup water, juice

Cider Vinegar is one ingredient you can use to keep your body well-balanced.

Add one tablespoon Worcestershire sauce

· 1/2 teaspoon Dijon mustard 2 teaspoons mayonnaise

Half a teaspoon of onion powder.

· 2 teaspoons hot sauce, or as much as you want:)

Preparation

Active: 15 m

Ready In: 40 Minutes

Put all the ingredients except honey in a heavy medium saucepan; bring the mixture to a simmer over medium heat. Remove from the heat, stir in the honey, and stir to blend.

Nutrition information

Ø Serving size: 2 Tbsp.

When we eat this bar our per-serving value is 65 calories. In general, per-serving values of bars with many added sugars and little to no fiber will be higher than this one.

Ø Capsule Servings: 1 or 200

All-American BBQ Sauce

MAPLE PECAN TART WITH DRIED CHERRIES.

Ingredients

· 1 large egg white

Debbie, In 3 tablespoons of butter, melted (using the word in the same position), distribute the 3 tablespoons of unsalted butter.

· 2 tablespoons canola oil

Breakfast: 1 tablespoon of water

¼ cup chopped pecans

· 1 tablespoon sugar

1 cup plus 2 tablespoons

½ teaspoon salt.

· 2 large eggs

Maple syrup is a natural sweetener, and since the ancient Greeks, people have loved it on various foods like breads and pastries.

¼ cup brown sugar

· 2 teaspoons dark rum (optional)

2 1/2 cups dried cranberries

Preparation

Active: 40 m

Ready in: 2 hours and 15 minutes.

· Preheat the oven to 400°F. Starting with a thin layer of dough, cover the bottom of a tart pan by pressing the dough into the bottom, all around, until 1/

Combine the egg yolk, butter, oil, and water in a small bowl. Cook the nut add with the sugar until it reaches a consistency like coarse meal. Add flour and a bit of salt and pulse until the mixture is combined. Drizzle the oil-yolk mixture through the feed tube while pulsing and pulse just until the mixture is combined.

· Take a piece of the crisp, dry crust, and fold it in half. Repeat with the remaining crust, rolling it out on a flat work surface and then rolling it up to form a cigar shape.

· Here's how to create your own breakfast sandwiches. Beat two eggs and add 2 tablespoons of maple syrup and 1 tablespoon of brown sugar. Mix in the rum and salt and vanilla extract if you'd like. Load half of the egg mixture between slices of buttered bread. Using a slotted spoon, top the egg mixture with half of the cherry mixture. Top with the remaining bread and press gently so the egg mixture

· Remove the crust from the oven. Reduce the oven temperature to 350 degrees.

On this occasion, the court tried to define the term "normies" – a term used to describe those who view alcohol, by far the most popular alcoholic beverage in Italy, as a "fast-food" product. The court also decided that the term "normies" should be seen as a "sexist,

Let the tart cool on a wire rack for 5-10 minutes then gently remove the sides of the pan. Use a butter knife to remove the sides of the pan if it sticks to the pan and the tart resists. Cool on a wire rack for 10-30 minutes.

Make Ahead Tip: Take your casserole out of the refrigerator 30 minutes before serving. It will be ready to eat then.

Here is the 9-inch tart pan with a removable bottom

Use a Rimmed Baking sheet to easily throw food messes and cleanup. Line it with a layer of foil before each usage to avoid cleanup. And keep it in perfect shape with a layer of foil between uses.

Nutrition information

Serving size: 1 slice

Per serving: 353 calories; 22 grams of fat (4 grams sat); 2 grams of fiber; 36 grams of carbohydrates; 5 grams protein; 53 mg of folate; 65 mg of cholesterol; 21 grams of sugars; 20 grams of added sugars; 348 IU vitamin A; 0 mg of vitamin C; 47 mg of calcium;

Vitamin D3: 0.5 µg (5000 IU)

1 starch 1½ other carbohydrate 4 fat

MAPLE PECAN ACAI TART WITH DRIED CHERRIES

SWEET SOUTHERN EGG SALAD

Ingredients

· 3 tablespoons nonfat plain yogurt 3 tablespoons nonfat plain yogurt

· three tablespoons low-fat mayonnaise

· · Mustard ·

Cinnamon and cinnamon stars can be added to muffins, pancakes or waffles as an extra flavoring. They can also be added to oatmeal as a topping. Take a small amount

Being healthy doesn't mean feeding on high-salt products

· 8 eggs

· Half a cup thinly sliced celery

· A: My first and only thought is to paraphrase, given the context, "her life spanned years of incredible change for women as they gained more rights than

· 1 tablespoon chopped sweet onion And I would provide a sample of a creative way to rewrite the text as was suggested by

Preparation

Active: 15 m

15 Meters in

· ·

· Wash the bell peppers. Cut them open, and removing the seeds, boil in water for 10 minutes or until soft, then drain. Remove the peppers from the water and pat them dry with paper towel.

Make Ahead Tip: Cover and refrigerate for up to 2 days.

Tips for hard-boiling eggs. Cover eggs with water. Bring to a boil over medium-high heat. Reduce heat to low. Cook for 10 minutes. Remove from heat, drain off boiling water and cover with ice-cold water. Let stand for 5 minutes. Peel eggs and store in the refrigerator.

Nutrition information

about 1 to 2 cup.

per serving: 15 g calories; 1 g fat; 0 g fiber; 6 g carbohydrates; 11 g protein; 22 mcg folate; 140 mg cholesterol; 3 g sugars; 1 g added sugars; 5 IU vitamin A; You could just as well paste the entire unedited text in it's original location without

Ø Carbohydrate Servings: ½

Her BMR was Ø area.

CHOW DOW EGG SALAD

Sardines noodles

Ingredients

¼ cup honey

2 teaspoons lime fresh.

·

· 1 teaspoon Indian milds powder

· ¼ teaspoon onion powder separated

1 pork tenderloin (1-1¼ pounds), trimmed.

· A pinch of salt

· 2 tablespoons extra-virgin olive virgin But after adding the olive oil to the dish, it looked

There's a thick richness to broth that's kind of nice. I didn't realize just how good a broth can be.

· ½ cup of water

· ½ cup quick grits

Freshly ground pepper can be stirred into a wet, cold dough. A: The essence of the original is contained in the following quote Is it too late to

· ½ cup shredded extra-sharp Cheddar cheese

·2 scallions, sliced

Preparation

Active: 30 m

Take a 30 minute break

Heat oven to 425°F.

Honey, lime juice, soy sauce, and onion powder are mixed together in a small bowl.

Sprinkle pork with salt and granulated onion. Heat oil in a medium skillet over high heat. Sear the pork until brown on all sides and use metal tongs to transfer the pork to the oven. Bake the pork until done, at least 4 to 5 minutes.

... [Roast the pork until the temperature reaches 145°F, throw away the skillet, and serve.]

While, the chef cooked the grits in a medium-sized saucepan, he promptly whisked in broth to add flavor and then seasoned the grits with pepper. After that, cover the grits to keep warm.

Slice the pork. Make sure to place the pork in a bowl, put it in the skillet and place the pig in the skillet. Make sure to pour any glaze left over the pork.

People who are unable to tolerate wheat or gluten can use soy sauces that are labeled "gluten-free" since these soy sauces could contain wheat or other gluten-containing sweeteners and flavorings.

Nutrition information

Ø Serving Size: 3 oz pork and ½ cup grits

The per serving is: 402 calories; 14 g fat; 1 g fiber; 37 g\\ carbohydrates; and 32 g protein. The total amount of carbohydrates is a little more than the recommended 45 grams and the fiber is a little less than the recommended 1 gram.

2½ Servings of Carbohydrates

Fats are high in saturated fat, while proteins and carbo-hydrates are low in fat. It's important to eat a mixture of these foods to stay healthy.

grilled pork tenderloin with cheese grits

MUSTARD + DRIED CHERRIES

Ingredients

· The most natural state for a human being would be one of equilibrium. The human body is meant to be in balance when a person is away from food.

2 cups cider vinegar

1 tablespoon of honey

This recipe includes 1-inch round risotto or lentil salad with mustard

· ¼ teaspoon salt

¼/1teaspoon freshly ground pepper

Some canola oil (¾ cup).

Preparation

Active: 15 m

Ready In: 15 minutes

This recipe may take more time than people expect, but it is worth the effort. Add vinegar, good mustard, a sweet and some salt and pepper. Slowly drizzle in olive oil until the mixture thickens and becomes smooth. Serve at room temperature.

Of course, you're welcome to serve this chicken sooner or later. Or it will last for 2 days in the fridge, if you'd like.

Nutrition information

Ø Serving size: 2 tablespoons

A person could eat an individually wrapped pizza slice from Pizza Hut for the same amount of calories as a total meal from McDonald's for a whole day.

Ø Carbohydrate Servings: ½

Ø Exchanges: 2 fat

Honey Mustard-Vidalia Dipping Sauce

NUGGETS OF MUSCLE

Ingredients

· 2 oz reduced fat cream cheese, softened (¼ cup).

She liked a good bowl of pasta, preferably with a bit of cheese on top.

· Two cups shredded Monterey jack cheese

· 3 tablespoons low-fat mayonnaise

· 1

· 1 teaspoon grated onion

Add 1/8 teaspoon of garlic powder to make the sauce powdery.

Personal trainer

·

· cup finely chopped toasted pecans.

Preparation

Active: 30 m

Ready when it's 1 hour

· To make a cream cheese spread, Cube the cheese, combine it with mayonnaise, tomato, green peppers and onion. Season with salt and black pepper and overuse. Refrigerate for at least 30 minutes or place in the freezer until chilled thoroughly.

A homeowner discovered their cat was missing and they assumed it had been taken by a neighborly thief. The family then scoured the neighborhood with a police dog but were unable to locate the cat. After that, a neighbor offered to trade some chocolate chip cookies for

· · Try the cheese balls at room temperature or iced.

Cook 1 to 2 days ahead of time and then cool and refrigerate. Bake the balls through Step 10 up to 3 days ahead. Cool and refrigerate the finished balls.

To toast nuts, spread on a cookie sheet and bake at 350°F. Stir after 7 to 9 minutes until fragrant.

Nutrition information

Ø

Per serving: ◦ 66 calories ◦ 6 grams of fat (2g saturated fat) ◦ 0 grams of fiber ◦ 3 grams of carbs ◦ 1 gram of protein ◦ 2 mcg of folate ◦ 12mg of cholesterol ◦ 0 grams of sugar ◦ 0 grams of added

Ø Carbohydrate Servings: 0

Ø Exchanges: 1 fat

NUTTY PIMIENTO CHEESE BALLS

SUMMER SUCCOTASH SALAD

Ingredients

2 cups shelled unsalted butter beans. Use the fresh, frozen, or baby lima beans.

· 4 tablespoons oil, divided/evenly

· . Original: · Baking powder and salt, to taste Paraphrase: 1 tsp cornstarch, 1/2 tsp baking powder, 1/2 tsp salt

· Can

· · chopped 1 small yellow squash

· 1 small zucchini, chopped and mixed with 2 eggs 1/2 bag dry pasta (that is not al dente) 1 tablespoon olive oil

· · · Heat up a skillet that is wide enough to hold the tomato in one piece.

(Celery-tip conflicts. C counts as a vegetable) You may be interested in:

½ a cup of freshly cut basil.

· Crush 2 tablespoons of apple cider vinegar.

· 1 tablespoon Dijon mustard #~# Original: ·

· 1 / 2 teaspoon salt

Lightly, before adding salt, spices, you should taste.

Preparation

Active: 40 m

The activity takes about 1 hour.

Place beans in a large bowl of water. Bring to a boil. Reduce to a simmer. Add beans and partially cover. Cook until tender. Remove from the heat. Drain and discard the cooking liquid. Transfer to a medium serving bowl.

Transfer the roasted vegetables to a large bowl. Add the beans and let cool for at least 1 hour.

· Cool the beans, vegetables and summer tomatoes, celery and basil.

Using oil and vinegar, make a dressing from the raw ingredients. Season with salt and pepper. Drizzle the dressing over the succotash and toss to combine.

Over to you! Make Ahead Tip: To prepare this dish, remove the rack from the oven and proceed with Steps 3 and 4.

To remove the corn kernels from the cob, stand one corn ear on one end and then slice off all the kernels with a sharp knife. The kernels will drop from the cob for about ½ cup.

Nutrition information

About 3/4 cup

There are 150 calories in each serving. It is recommended you eat three (3) servings per day.

Ø Nutrition

Ø Carbohydrate Servings: 1½

Ø (Corn) Exchanges: ½ Starch, 1 Vegetable, 1 Fat

Summer succotash salad

COFFEE PANNA COTTA

Ingredients

Panna Cotta

· "just enough coffee for an espresso machine"

. . . 1 envelope unflavored gelatin (about 2¼ ~ teaspoons)

A cup of vanilla nonfat yogurt

1 cup of milk is required to meet your daily calcium needs.

2 teaspoons brandy

Obviously, this is just a test, but wait a minute; a scholar has sneaked into the test. He or she has some opinions and they have been written on the test paper

¼ teaspoon cinnamon, ground into a fine powder,...

· ⅓ cup of granulated sugar (depending on your length and the importance of the particular article).

· ½ cup whipping cream, chilled. Paraphrase: · ½ cup whipping cream, well chilled

Coffee-Brandy Sauce

· 1 cup brown sugar

You need 3 tablespoons of ground coffee.

- It may take a couple times to get a hang on

Preparation

Active: 30 m

Start 5 hour

To ready the panna cotta, place ½ cup hot coffee in a small heatproof double boiler. Sprinkle gelatin over the coffee; stir to mix. Let stand for 5 minutes.

First, mix the remaining cup of coffee, yogurt, milk, 2 teaspoons brandy, vanilla extract and cinnamon thoroughly in a medium bowl.

The caffeine-gelatin mixture must be microwaved to fully dissolve the gelatin, but don't let it boil than add sugar. Stir until smooth.

While whisking the gelatin mixture slowly into the yogurt, refrigerate the mixture, stirring occasionally, until it thickens slightly.

Whisk the cream with a wire whisk until it forms soft peaks. Beat the mixture into the yogurt mixture until smooth.

Hot sauce is typically quite spicy. The heat can be adjusted by adding or removing ingredients. Some recipes call for added spices, while others call for a milder flavor, there are even jalapeno or habanero varieties. Rumor is that recipes hailing from Cuba contain a special type of hot sauce more like super-sauce. The combination of brown sugar and coffee can then be added for extra taste if desired. The instructions for making the live spiced rum were not provided

Place the panna cottas into a bain-marie where they will be served hot. You will need to boil for 30-40 seconds to bring the mousse to a foamy consistency. Allow the mousse to cool for 3 minutes before serving. Add the sauce to the panna cottas and drape with the hot fluted round or brushed cup over the top. This mousse is lovely served in champagne cups, but

Make Ahead Tip: Keep covered and refrigerate panna cotta for up to 3 days. Warm up the sauce for a few seconds to use.

The Forex Exchange Curation Team demonstrated a variety of strategies for students to use to improve their foreign exchange trading.

Nutrition information

She poured the milk over a bowl of cereal. Each serving contains 181 calories. On the container, it says that there are no additional added sugars. She has seven grams of saturated fat. The information about calories and other ingredients can be found on the nutrition label.

Ø Carbohydrate Servings: 1½

You can have two or three - ½ cup fat-free milk, one other carbohydrate (such as rice, oats or bread), one fat; or ¼ cup

CPSIA information can be obtained
at www.ICGtesting.com
Printed in the USA
BVHW031235260722
643033BV00014B/927

9 781804 769942